BTEC First

Sport

For Performance, Exercise and
Fitness, and Outdoor Recreation

BTEC First
Sport

For Performance, Exercise and Fitness, and Outdoor Recreation

Jennifer Stafford-Brown, Simon Rea,
Lee Janaway and Chris Manley

Hodder Arnold

A MEMBER OF THE HODDER HEADLINE GROUP

endorsed by
edexcel

This high quality material is endorsed by Edexcel and has been through a rigorous quality assurance programme to ensure that it is a suitable companion to the specification for both learners and teachers. This does not mean that its contents will be used verbatim when setting examinations nor is it to be read as being the official specification – a copy of which is available at www.edexcel.org.uk

Orders: please contact Bookpoint Ltd, 130 Milton Park, Abingdon, Oxon OX14 4SB. Telephone: (44) 01235 827720. Fax: (44) 01235 400454. Lines are open from 9.00–5.00, Monday to Saturday, with a 24 hour message answering service. You can also order through our website www.hoddereducation.co.uk

If you have any comments to make about this, or any of our other titles, please send them to educationenquiries@hodder.co.uk

British Library Cataloguing in Publication Data
A catalogue record for this title is available from the British Library

ISBN-10: 0 340 92604 X
ISBN-13: 978 0 340 92604 8

First Edition Published 2006
Impression number   10 9 8 7 6 5 4 3
Year   2011 2010 2009 2008 2007 2006

Cover photo by Sean Justice /Photonica /Getty Images
Artwork by Tony Jones, Art Construction

Typeset in 12/14 Minion by Charon Tec Ltd, Chennai, India
www.charontec.com

Printed in Italy for Hodder Arnold, an imprint of Hodder Education, a member of the Hodder Headline Group, 338 Euston Road, London NW1 3BH.

Contents

Acknowledgements

I would like to thank the following people for their hard work, advice and/or information that helped make this book possible: my co-authors, Tamsin and the Hodder publishing team, colleagues from Edexcel and Vicki and Sean McQuaid. Particular thanks go out to my husband, daughter, baby son and parents for their love, continued support and understanding.
Jennifer Stafford-Brown

Many thanks to the sports staff and students at Uxbridge College and also my fellow writers for their help and inspiration during writing. Special love and thanks to my family and in particular my niece and nephews: Rebecca; James; Eddie; Harry and William - you bring me so much fun and joy. Finally to my three brilliant friends, Carl, Joanne and Gemma for all the laughter, love and support when I need it.
Simon Rea

I would like to thank my team and students at North Hertfordshire College for their inspiration and hard work, especially Gordon Barr and James Luscombe. I would also like to thank my wife Vicky and parents John and Sue for supporting me in my career and Simon Rea for his guidance over the years and giving me the chance to work in education.
Lee Janaway

I would like to thank all of those who helped me, particularly Michelle and to my family, Jo, and our very special daughter Ella who makes my day every day.
Chris Manley

The authors and publishers would like to thank the following for the permission to use the following photographs in this volume:

p14 Alamy/Phototake Inc, **p18** SPL/Matt Meadows, Peter Arnold INC., **p23** (left) Getty Images/Jonathan Daniel (right) Rex Features/ SIPA Press, **p28** (left) Action Plus (right) Corbis/Pete Leonard/Zefa, **p29** SPL/Dr P.Marazzi, **p31** SPL/Lea Paterson, **p33** Alamy/Ace Stock Ltd, **p39** Rex Features, Joe Pepler, **p40** (top) Action Plus/Steve Bardens (bottom) Courtesy Health and Safety Commission, **p41** Courtesy Health and Safety Executive, **p42** Rex Features, **p58** Getty Images/Justine Pumfrey, **p66** Corbis/Stephen Hird/Reuters, **p81** SPL/Matthew Munro, **p82** Getty Images/Scott Boehm, **p89** Rex Features/Yann Feron, **p100** Rex Features, **p101** Corbis/Emely/Zefa, **p102** (left) Getty/Stu Forster (right) **pp108, 109, 128, 253** Action Plus/Neil Tingle, **p112** Empics/Gareth Copley/PA, **p113** Rex Features, **p122** Getty Images/AFP/Ian Stewart, **p123** Getty Images, **p125** Rex Features/Peter Burian, **pp126, 127, 283** John Cleare/Mountain Camera, **p128** Action Plus, Steve Bardens, **p130** (left) Courtesy Adventure Activities Licensing Authority (right) Courtesy Countryside Agency, **p132** (left) Courtesy British Orienteering Federation (right) Courtesy British Canoe Union, **p133** (top) Courtesy Snowsport, England (bottom) Courtesy Duke of Edinburgh Award Scheme, **p137** Courtesy Countryside Agency, **p141** Getty Images/Jesse D. Garrabrant, **pp148, 193** Action Plus/Glyn Kirk, **p149** Getty Images/Hamish Blair, **p151** Rex Features, SIPA Press, **p161** Getty Images/AFP/Farjana K.Godhuly, **p167** Alamy/© Stock Connection Distribution, **p172** Rex Features, Eddie Keogh, **p173** Getty Images, Thomas Coex, **p174** Empics/Olivier Douliery/ABACA, **p232** Getty Images/Harry How, **p238** Alamy/ Dattatreya, **p274** Getty Images/Altrendo, **p276** Rex Features/Image Source, **p284** Corbis/John Norris, **p285** Corbis/John Stewart, **p287** Corbis/ Karl Weatherly, **p292** Courtesy Camelbak, **p295** Rex Features/Shout, **p308** SPL/Steve Allen, **p309** Alamy/Jason Friend, **p313** Corbis/Ashley Cooper, **p316** Alamy/StockShot

Core Units

1

This chapter explores the foundations of anatomy and physiology. It covers the structure and function of the skeletal system, the muscular system, the cardiovascular system and the respiratory system. The short and long-term effects of exercise on each of these systems will also be explored. An outline of the aerobic and anaerobic energy systems will be given, together with the energy requirements of a range of sports.

Goal

By the end of this chapter you will:

- Know about the function and structure of the skeleton and how it is affected by exercise
- Know about the muscular system of the body and how it is affected by exercise
- Understand the respiratory system and how it is affected by exercise
- Understand the cardiovascular system and how it is affected by exercise
- Know about the fundamentals of the energy systems.

The skeleton

Function of the skeleton

There are five main functions that the skeleton performs: shape, movement, protection, blood production and mineral storage.

Shape

Without a skeleton we would not have the human form; we would be a shapeless structure like a jelly on the floor. Our skeleton forms a frame under the skin to which muscles attach and within which internal organs can sit.

Movement

The skeleton is made up of lots of bones that are connected by joints that allow different degrees of movement. Muscles are then attached to these bones which pull on them and produce movement.

Protection

Internal organs are delicate in comparison to bones and muscles, and they would not be able to withstand the many everyday stresses we place on our body unless they were protected by the skeleton. Various areas of the skeleton protect different vital organs, for example the ribs and sternum protect the heart and lungs, the brain is protected by the cranium, the vertebral column protects the spinal cord and in pregnant females the pelvis protects the developing foetus.

Blood production

Red bone marrow makes red and white blood cells. The centres of some bones in the skeleton contain red bone marrow and therefore are the site of blood production. The main bones that are responsible for blood production are the sternum, vertebral column and the pelvic girdle.

Mineral storage

The bones in the skeleton store minerals, which include phosphorus and calcium, the main and most important one being calcium. The calcium in our bones is largely responsible for ensuring they remain hard and are able to withstand impact, i.e. they do not break when we fall over. As our bones are continually being broken down and replaced, we require a constant supply of calcium to ensure the 'new' bones are tough and durable.

Bone structure

Figure 1.1 shows the different components of a bone.

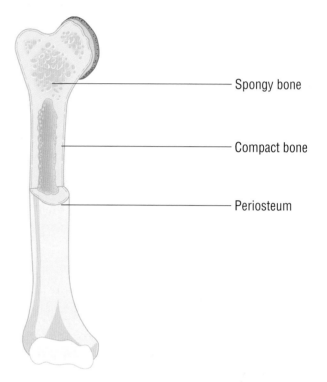

Fig. 1.1   Long bone

Periosteum

This is the thin outer layer of the bone. It contains nerves and blood vessels that feed the bone.

Spongy bone

Spongy bone is found inside compact bone and is full of tiny holes.

Compact bone

Compact bone is hard and gives bones their rigidity.

Cancellous bone

Cancellous bone lies in layers within the compact bone. It has a honeycomb appearance (like the inside of a Crunchie bar or Maltesers) and is not quite as hard as compact bone.

Bone marrow

Bone marrow is a jelly-like substance and is located centrally within certain bones. The bone marrow produces new blood cells. In many bones, the cancellous bone protects the inner-most part of the bone, the bone marrow.

Bone growth

When you were growing in your mother's womb, most of your skeleton was made from cartilage. As you grow older, this cartilage develops into bone which is much firmer and tougher than cartilage.

Ossification: Ossification is the process of cartilage turning into bone.

The process of ossification continues until we are fully grown. Towards the ends of our bones there are areas which contain cartilage and are called 'growth plates'. The cartilage is turned into bone and the bone continues to grow until we are adults.

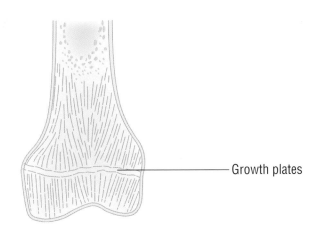

Growth plates

Fig. 1.2 Bone with growth plates

Major bones

You are born with around 350 bones. However, as you grow, some of these bones join together to form one bone. Once you become an adult your skeleton will consist of 206 bones.

Skull

The skull consists of the cranium that protects the brain and facial bones, which include the upper and lower jaw and other facial structures.

Sternum (breast bone)

This is located in the middle of the chest.

Ribs

Adults have 12 pairs of ribs. The ribs are flat bones that are joined to the sternum to form a protective cage around the heart and lungs.

Clavicle (collar bone)

This bone connects the upper arm to the trunk of the body. One end is connected to the sternum (breast bone) and the other is connected to the scapula (shoulder blade).

Scapula (shoulder blade)

This bone is situated on the back of the body.

Arm

This consists of three bones: the humerus (upper arm), the radius and the ulna (lower arm).

Pelvis (hips)

The pelvis protects and supports the lower internal organs, including the bladder, the reproductive organs and also, in pregnant women, the developing foetus.

Leg

The leg consists of four bones: the femur (thigh bone), tibia (shin bone), fibula (lower leg) and patella (kneecap).

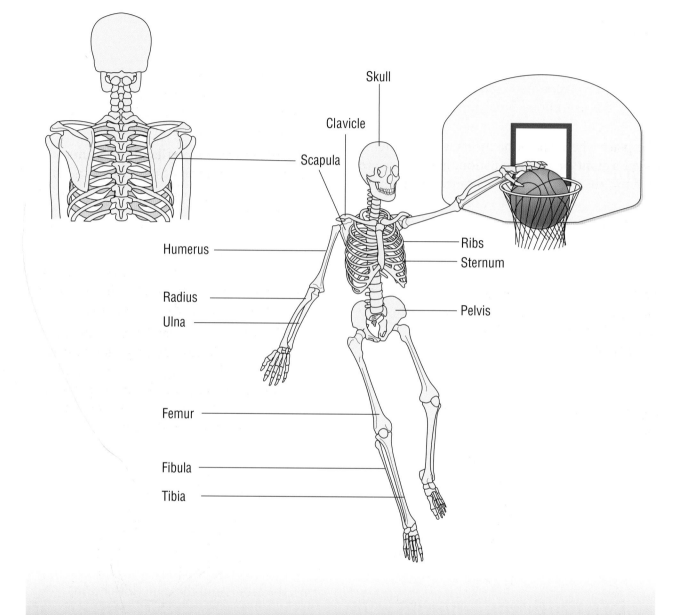

Fig. 1.3   Major bones of the body

Key learning points

- The functions of the skeleton are shape, movement, protection, blood production and mineral storage.

- A bone is made up of a periosteum, compact bone, cancellous bone and bone marrow.

- Bones grow at their growth plates.

Joints

definition

Joint: A joint is the place where one bone meets with another.

The place where one bone meets with another is called a joint or an articulation, and bones are held together by strong bands called ligaments.

definition

Ligament: A ligament joins bones to other bones.

Some of these joints allow a great deal of movement, for example your shoulder joint. However, some joints allow very little movement or no movement at all.

Structure of a joint

Figure 1.4 below shows the structure of a synovial joint.

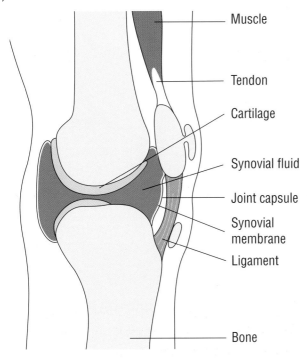

- Muscle
- Tendon
- Cartilage
- Synovial fluid
- Joint capsule
- Synovial membrane
- Ligament
- Bone

Fig. 1.4 Structure of a synovial joint

Types of joint

Joints are put into one of three categories:

1 **Fixed/immoveable joints** – (also sometimes called fibrous) – as the name suggests, these joints allow no movement. These types of joints can be found in the skull.

2 **Slightly moveable/cartilaginous joints** – these allow a little bit of movement and are linked by cartilage. These kinds of joints can be found between the vertebrae in your spine and also between the ribs and the sternum.

3 **Freely moveable/synovial joints** – there are six types of these joints and all allow varying degrees of movement: hinge, ball and socket, pivot, condyloid, saddle and gliding.

- *Hinge joint* – these can be found in your elbows and knees, and they allow you to bend and then straighten your arms and legs. Hinge joints are like the hinges on a door, and allow you to bend your arms and legs in only one direction.

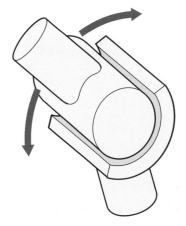

Fig. 1.5 Hinge joint

- *Ball and socket joint* – these types of joint can be found at your shoulders and hips and allow lots of movement in every direction. A ball and socket joint is made up of a round end of one bone that fits into a small cup-like area of another bone.

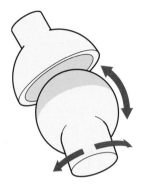

Fig. 1.6   Ball and socket joint

- *Pivot joint* – this joint can be found in your neck. It only allows rotational movement, for example it allows you to move your head from side to side as if you were saying 'no'.

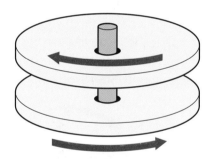

Fig. 1.7   Pivot joint

- *Condyloid joint* – this type of joint can be found at the wrist. It allows movement in two planes. It allows you to bend and straighten the joint, and move it from side to side.

- *Saddle joint* – this type of joint can only be found in your thumbs. It allows the joint to move in two planes, backwards and forwards, and from side to side.

- *Gliding joint* – this type of joint can be found in the carpal bones of the hand. These types of joints occur between the surfaces of two flat bones. They allow very limited movement in a range of directions.

Fig. 1.8   Condyloid joint

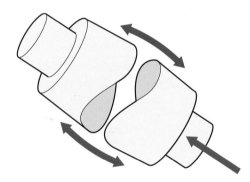

Fig. 1.9   Saddle joint

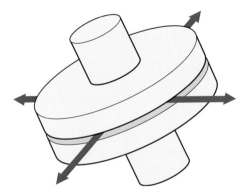

Fig. 1.10   Gliding joint

Types of joint movement

There is a number of different types of joint movement:

- **Flexion** – this means bending the joint. This occurs at the knee when one is preparing to kick a football.

● **Extension** – this means straightening the joint. This occurs at the elbow when one is shooting in netball.

● **Adduction** – this means movement towards the body. This occurs at the shoulder when one is in the pulling phase of the breast stroke.

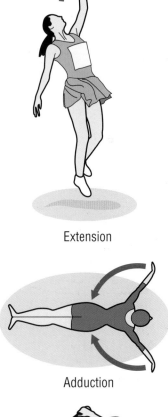

Extension

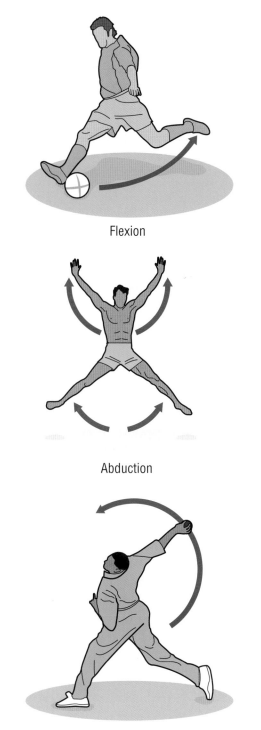

Flexion

Abduction

Circumduction

Adduction

Rotation

- **Abduction** – this means movement away from the body. This occurs at the hip during a star jump.

- **Circumduction** – this means that the limb moves in a circle. This occurs at the shoulder joint during an overarm bowl in cricket.

- **Rotation** – this means that the limb moves in a circular movement towards the middle of the body. This occurs in the hip while performing a drive shot in golf.

Key learning points

There are three categories of joint: fixed, slightly moveable and moveable/synovial.

Type of joint	Type of movement	Examples in the body
Hinge joint	Flexion and extension	Elbow, knee
Ball and socket	Flexion and extension Abduction and adduction Circumduction and rotation	Hips and shoulders
Pivot	Rotation	Neck
Condyloid	Flexion and extension Abduction and adduction	Wrist
Saddle	Flexion and extension Abduction and adduction	Thumb
Gliding joint	Limited movement in all directions	Carpals

Student activity

Give examples of other sporting movements in which you would see the sports person perform each of the above types of movement.

Effects of exercise on the skeletal system

definition

Weight-bearing exercise: A weight-bearing exercise is where we are using our body weight as a form of resistance, e.g walking, running etc.

Our skeleton responds to weight-bearing exercise or resistance exercise by becoming stronger and more able to withstand impact, which means we are less likely to break a bone if we fall over. This occurs because the stimulation of exercise means we increase the mineral content within our bones, which makes them harder and stronger. Exercise also has an effect on our joints by increasing the thickness of cartilage at the ends of the bones and increasing the production of synovial fluid. This will have the effect of making our joints stronger and we are therefore less likely to suffer from a joint injury.

Student activity

ossification	calcium	flexion	the leg	ball and socket
ribs	abduction	bone marrow	pivot	immovable

Choose a word from the boxes above to answer the following questions:

1 What is the main mineral stored in bones?
2 Where are blood cells produced?
3 Which bones protect the heart and lungs?
4 Which limb consists of four bones?
5 What is the name given to the process of cartilage turning into bone?
6 A hinge joint is shaped to allow which type of movement to take place?

7 Which term describes movement away from the body?
8 This type of joint can be found in the neck.
9 This type of joint can be found in the skull.
10 This type of synovial joint allows the greatest range of movement.

The muscular system

Types of muscle tissue

There are three types of muscle tissue: smooth, skeletal and cardiac.

Smooth muscles

Smooth muscles are also called involuntary muscles. You cannot consciously control this type of muscle; your brain and body tell these muscles what to do without you even having to think about it. Smooth muscle can be found all over your body, for example in your digestive system, in your bladder and in your eyes.

Cardiac muscle

The heart is made up of cardiac muscle (also known as the myocardium). Cardiac muscle is also called an involuntary muscle as it contracts without you consciously having to control it. Cardiac muscle consists of specialised fibres which do not tire.

Skeletal muscle

You are all probably familiar with this type of muscle as they are responsible for allowing us to move and take part in sports. As you know, if you 'work out' you will gain good muscle tone and shape and it is this skeletal muscle you are training. This type of muscle is also known as striated muscle, which basically means that if you were to look at it under a microscope you would see that it has a striped appearance.

Skeletal muscles are also known as voluntary muscles. This means you can control what they do, so if you want to kick a ball, you have to think about it and this will make your skeletal muscles contract to allow the movement to happen.

Key learning points

- There are three types of muscle tissue: smooth, skeletal and cardiac.
- Smooth muscles and cardiac muscles are involuntary muscle.
- Skeletal muscles are voluntary muscle.

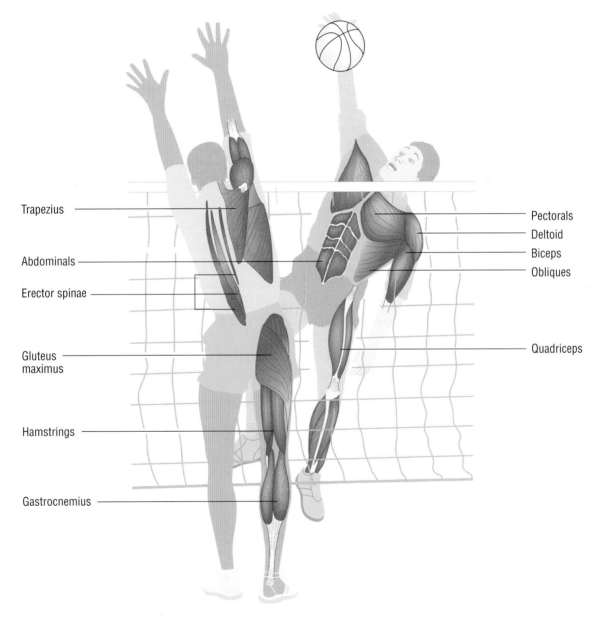

Trapezius

Abdominals

Erector spinae

Gluteus maximus

Hamstrings

Gastrocnemius

Pectorals

Deltoid

Biceps

Obliques

Quadriceps

Fig. 1.11   The major muscles of the body, front and back

Major muscles

Figure 1.11 shows the major muscles that can be found in the human body.

Muscle movement

Tendons are responsible for joining skeletal muscles to your skeleton.

Tendons: Tendons join muscles to the skeleton.

Tendons are cords made of tough tissue, and they work to connect muscle to bones. When the muscle contracts, it pulls on the tendon which in turn pulls on the bone and makes the bone move.

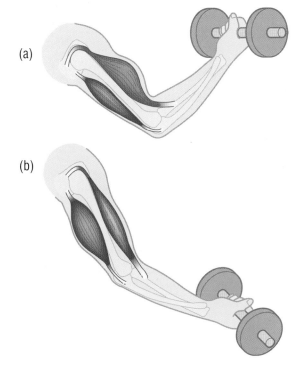

(a)

(b)

Fig. 1.12 The biceps and triceps in (a) upwards and (b) downwards phase of bicep curl

Muscles can only produce a pulling movement, so each muscle has a 'partner' which can return the body part back to its original position. These are called antagonistic muscle pairs.

Antagonistic muscle pairs: In antagonistic muscle pairs, as one muscle contracts the other relaxes.

Student activity

Copy out the table below, then place the correct muscle next to its partner.

Biceps	Quadriceps
Hamstrings	Erector spinae
Abdominals	Trapezius
Pectorals	Triceps

There are three main types of muscle contraction:

1 Concentric contraction

2 Eccentric contraction

3 Isometric contraction.

Concentric contraction

This is the main type of muscle contraction. In this type of contraction, the muscle gets shorter and the two ends of the muscle move closer together.

Eccentric contraction

In this type of muscle contraction, the muscle actually increases in length while still producing tension. The two ends of the muscle move further apart. For example, in the lowering phase of a bicep curl, the biceps are working eccentrically to control the lowering of the weight.

Fig. 1.13 Knee flexion

Fig. 1.14 Eccentric contraction

Isometric contraction

In this type of contraction, the muscle actually stays the same length, so there is no movement of the muscle or body part that is attached, e.g. the quadriceps during a ski squat.

Fig. 1.15 Isometric contraction

Student activity

Think of three other sporting examples for each type of muscle contraction.

Effects of exercise on the muscular system

If you exercise with some sort of resistance, e.g. weights, dyna band, body weight as in press-ups, it will stress the skeletal muscle. This actually results in parts of the muscle breaking. The more you stress the muscle with heavier weights, the more the muscle breaks down. After having rested and eaten the right foods, the body then starts to repair itself and will actually mend the muscle tissue and make it bigger and better than before. If you continue this process, the muscle tissue will keep getting bigger, which will result in an increase in your muscle size – this is called hypertrophy.

Hypertrophy: Hypertrophy is an increase in the size of skeletal muscle.

definition

The respiratory system

The respiratory system is responsible for transporting the oxygen from the air we breathe into our body. Our body uses this oxygen in combination with the food we have eaten to produce energy. This energy is then used to keep us alive by supplying our heart with energy to keep beating and pumping blood around the body, and this in turn allows us to move and take part in sports and many other different types of activities.

Structure of the respiratory system

The respiratory system is basically made up of a system of tubes and muscles that allows us to breathe air in from the surrounding atmosphere and take it down into our lungs.

1   Air enters the body through the mouth and nose.

2   Air passes over the epiglottis. The epiglottis closes over the trachea (also known as the wind pipe) when we swallow food, to stop the food going down 'the wrong way' into our trachea and down into our lungs.

3   The air passes down into the trachea. If you reach up to the front of your neck, you will feel the trachea. The trachea is surrounded by horseshoe-shaped pieces of cartilage which keep it open.

4   The air passes down into two bronchi.

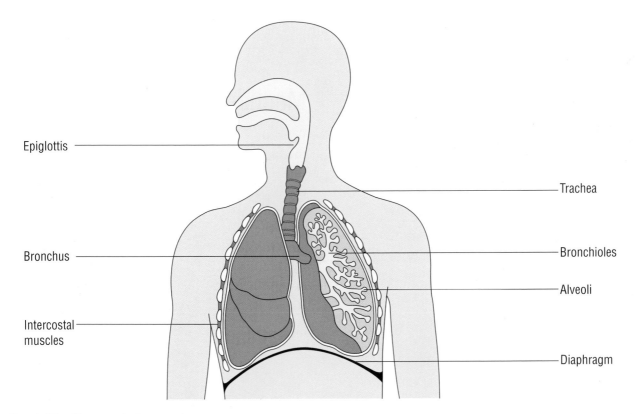

Fig. 1.16   The respiratory system

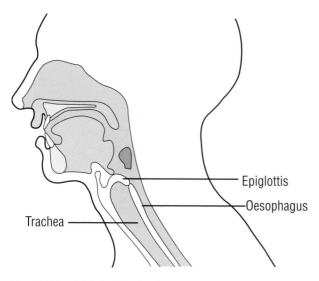

Fig. 1.17   Epiglottis closing over trachea allowing food down oesophagus

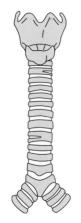

Fig. 1.18   Trachea with horseshoe-shaped cartilage

5   Air passes through the bronchi, which then divide into smaller tubes called bronchioles.

6   At the end of the bronchioles, the air reaches the alveoli, which is where the 'action happens'. The alveoli are microscopic air sacs. They have very thin walls, and are surrounded by capillaries.

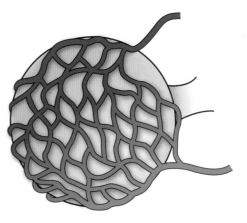

Fig. 1.19   Alveoli

The respiratory system also includes two types of muscles which work to move air into and out of the lungs.

- The diaphragm is a sheet of muscle which runs along the bottom of the lungs.
- The intercostal muscles are found between the ribs (if you enjoy eating spare ribs you are actually eating the intercostal muscles).

Mechanism of breathing

Breathing is the term given to inhaling air into the lungs and then exhaling it. The process basically works on the principle of making the thoracic cavity (chest) larger, which decreases the pressure of air within the lungs. The surrounding air is then at a higher pressure, which means that air is forced into the lungs. Then the thoracic cavity is returned to its original size, which forces air out of the lungs.

Breathing in (inhalation)

At rest
The diaphragm contracts and moves downwards. This results in an increase in the size of the thoracic cavity and air is forced into the lungs.

Exercise

During exercise, the diaphragm and intercostal muscles contract, which makes the ribs move upwards and outwards and results in more air being taken into the lungs.

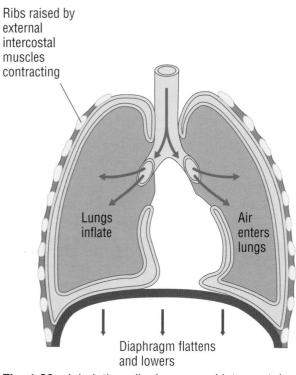

Ribs raised by external intercostal muscles contracting

Lungs inflate

Air enters lungs

Diaphragm flattens and lowers

Fig. 1.20 Inhalation, diaphragm and intercostal muscles

Breathing out (exhalation)

At rest

The diaphragm relaxes and returns upwards to a domed position. The thoracic cavity gets smaller, which results in an increase in air pressure within the lungs so that air is breathed out of the lungs.

Exercise

During exercise, the intercostal muscles contract to help decrease the size of the thoracic cavity and this results in a more forcible breathing out.

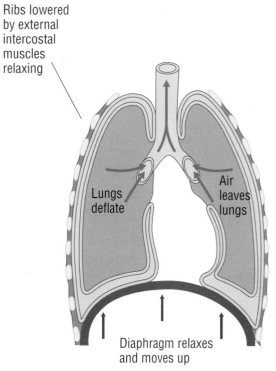

Ribs lowered by external intercostal muscles relaxing

Lungs deflate

Air leaves lungs

Diaphragm relaxes and moves up

Fig. 1.21 Exhalation, diaphragm and intercostal muscles

Student activity

Explain how breathing in and out changes when you are at rest and when you are exercising.

Gaseous exchange

Gaseous exchange: In the lungs, oxygen is taken into the blood and carbon dioxide is breathed out.

The oxygen from the air we have breathed in passes through the walls of the alveoli, into the surrounding capillaries and enters the bloodstream. In exchange for this oxygen, carbon dioxide passes out of the bloodstream through the capillaries and enters the alveoli. This carbon dioxide is then breathed out of the body.

Asthma

Asthma makes the tubes leading into the lungs smaller, which makes it harder to get air into and out of the lungs.

Smoking

If you smoke, the tar from your cigarette or cigar will start to block the alveoli in the lungs and eventually stop them functioning properly. The more you smoke, the more alveoli will be affected, which could also result in lung disease.

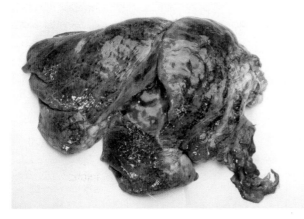

Lungs of a smoker

Effects of exercise on the respiratory system

Taking part in aerobic exercise will increase your breathing rate so that you can take more oxygen into the body and get rid of the excess carbon dioxide. If you take part in regular aerobic exercise it will train the lungs by increasing the lung capacity.

> **Lung capacity:** Lung capacity is the total amount of air your lungs can hold.

definition

Student activity

- Count your breathing rate at rest for one minute.
- Take part in one minute of aerobic exercise and count your breathing rate again.
- Explain why there is a difference between the two breathing rates.

Key learning points

- Air travels into the body through the mouth and nose, down the trachea and into the bronchus. It then passes into the bronchioles and down into the alveoli. In the alveoli gaseous exchange takes place which takes oxygen into the body and passes carbon dioxide out of the body.
- The diaphragm and intercostal muscles contract to allow you to breathe in and out.

The cardiovascular system

Function of the cardiovascular system

The cardiovascular system is made up of the heart and all the blood vessels that take blood to and from all parts of the body. It is responsible for delivering oxygen and nutrients to every part of our body. It carries hormones to different parts of the body, and takes away waste products such as carbon dioxide and lactic acid. The cardiovascular system helps to maintain body temperature by re-directing blood to the surface of the skin when we are hot (that's why your face turns red when you are hot, because blood vessels close to the surface of the skin open up to try and cool the body down).

The heart

Structure of the heart

The inside of the heart is hollow and is made up of four different hollow areas called chambers. The top two chambers are called atria and the bottom two are called ventricles. The atria receive blood from the body and the ventricles are responsible for pumping the blood out of the heart. The heart is divided into two sides, the right and the left side, by a wall of muscle called the septum.

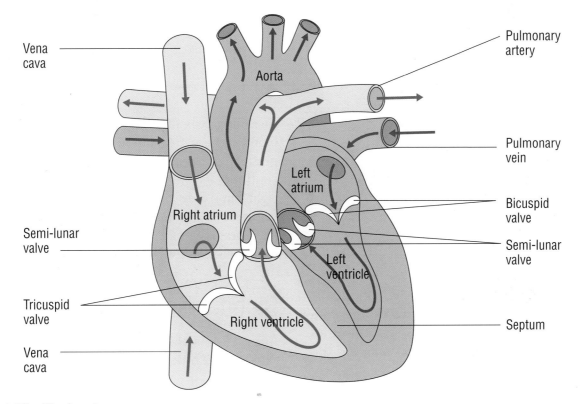

Fig. 1.22   The heart

Blood-flow through the heart

Blood flows through the heart and around the body in one direction. This one-way 'street' is maintained by special valves placed within the heart.

The heart is sometimes called a 'double pump' because the right-hand side of the heart pumps blood to the lungs and the left-hand side of the heart pumps blood to the body.

The heart as a double pump

Right-hand side

1 When the heart is relaxed, deoxygenated blood from the body enters the heart via the venae cavae.

2 Blood enters the right atria.

3 The right atria contracts (tightens) and pushes blood down through the tricuspid valve and into the right ventricle.

4 The right ventricle contracts, the tricuspid valve closes and blood is pushed up and out of the heart through the semilunar valve and into the pulmonary artery which takes the blood to the lungs.

5 The heart relaxes and the semilunar valves close to prevent blood flowing back into the heart.

Left-hand side

1 When the heart is relaxed, oxygenated blood from the lungs enters via the pulmonary vein.

2 Blood enters the left atria.

3 The left atria contracts (tightens) and pushes blood down through the bicuspid valve and into the left ventricle.

4 The left ventricle contracts and the bicuspid valve closes. Blood is then pushed up and out of the heart through the semilunar valve and into the aorta which takes blood to the rest of the body.

5 The heart relaxes and the semilunar valves close to prevent blood flowing back into the heart.

Student activity

In your own words, give an account of how blood travels through the heart, around the body and then to the lungs. Name all the major blood vessels that the blood travels through.

Function of the heart

All of your body cells need a steady and constant supply of oxygen. Blood is responsible for delivering oxygen to all the body's cells and this blood is pumped around the body and to the lungs by the heart. The left-hand side of your heart pumps the oxygenated blood to the body.

The body cells then take the oxygen out of the blood and use it, and in so doing produce a waste product called carbon dioxide. The blood then continues its journey back to the heart, enters the right-hand side and is pumped out of the right ventricle to the lungs. At the lungs, the blood becomes oxygenated and the waste product carbon dioxide is 'unloaded' and breathed out.

Blood vessels

In order to make this journey, blood is carried through five different types of blood vessels:

1 Arteries

2 Arterioles